TOE TAPPIN' TRIVIA

The Country Music Book that Gets You Singin'

and Keeps You Guessin'

By Bret Nicholaus and Paul Lowrie
Published by Ballantine Books:

THE CONVERSATION PIECE
THE CHRISTMAS CONVERSATION PIECE
THE MOM & DAD CONVERSATION PIECE
THINK TWICE!
TOE TAPPIN' TRIVIA

Books published by The Ballantine Publishing Group are available at quantity discounts on bulk purchases for premium, educational, fund-raising, and special sales use. For details, please call 1-800-733-3000.

TOE TAPPIN' TRIVIA

The Country Music Book that Gets You Singin' and Keeps You Guessin'

Bret Nicholaus and Paul Lowrie

BALLANTINE BOOKS • NEW YORK

A Ballantine Book
Published by The Ballantine Publishing Group
Copyright © 1999 by Paul Lowrie and Bret Nicholaus

www.randomhouse.com/BB/

Library of Congress Catalog Card Number: 98-96935

ISBN 0-345-43370-X

Manufactured in the United States of America

First Edition: May 1999

10 9 8 7 6 5 4 3 2 1

☆ ☆ ☆

Introduction

So you think you know your country music, eh? Well, you're about to find out just how well you *do* know it! This one-of-a-kind collection of trivia questions is guaranteed to test and expand your knowledge of country songs in a truly entertaining way. But before we go any further, let us tell you what you *won't* find in this book: you won't find trivia questions asking you what year a song was written, who wrote it, or where it peaked on the charts; you won't find questions asking you to name the birthplace of a country superstar or the year in which they died; and you won't be asked what label a singer is on or the names of Garth Brooks' children. Because as interesting as all that may be, we know that that's not what really interests you, the country music fan. Being diehard fans of country music ourselves, we know that what *really* matters are the songs—the ones you call your radio station to request, the ones you wait all day to hear, the ones that make you run out to buy the CD.

It has always been said that every country song tells a story . . . and that's what this book is all about. Our research (which, while extensive, was quite fun) took us through hundreds and hundreds of songs and an equal number of great stories—the ones you've heard countless times as they're played over the airwaves. Well, now it's time for you to see how well you know those stories. Generally speaking, you'll be given the title of a popular country song and the artist who sings it. We then give you a question whose answer is found somewhere within that song's story. The answer may be the name of a gas station, a city in the Southwest, the time of night when the song's main character comes home . . . hundreds of possibilities. (There's even one question whose answer is Johnny Carson!) Occasionally, we'll turn it around and give you part of the story to see if you can guess the song's title. If you're like most of the people who helped us test this entertaining book, you will often have to sing your way into the song to get to the part that supplies the answer. In other words, you're going to have a lot of fun humming up—er, coming up with the answers. If you've got enough people, you may even want to form teams (that way, if one person can't get the answer, someone else on the team can help along). Whether alone or in a group, you've got hours and hours of excitement and pondering ahead of you.

Each trivia question is based on a song that falls into one of three categories: 1) it finished as a number-one single on the country charts; 2) it didn't go to the top but received (or still receives) heavy airplay; or 3) it received limited airplay but would be considered a classic by any true fan of that artist. (Approximately 95 percent of the questions are based on songs that fall into the first two categories listed.) The questions themselves are mixed together, but there is an index in the back of the book listing your favorite artists by first and last name and giving you the question numbers that feature a song by that particular singer. All your favorites are here: George Strait, Garth Brooks, Alan Jackson, Alabama, Brooks and Dunn, Reba McEntire, George Jones, Diamond Rio, Tim McGraw, The Judds . . . more than one hundred artists and groups in all! Obviously, because of time and space, we do not have a question for every chart-topper out there; nor were we able to include all the country singers who deserve mention. We have tried to be fair, however, and mention as many popular hits and singers as we can, giving the bigger artists more questions since you probably hear their songs the most. At any rate, this truly unique trivia book will tell you once and for all how well you, your friends, and your family know those great country songs. Just to get the brain juices flowing, here's a jump start: In the chart-topping George Strait hit "Check Yes or No," what is the name of the little schoolgirl mentioned in the beginning of the song? (The answer is in the back of the book with all the other answers.)

Special thanks: This book wouldn't have been possible without the clever writing of country music's songwriters. In truth, this book should be dedicated to all of them for their creative way with words. While we always hear and know the name of the person who sings the song, we rarely hear the name of the one (or ones) who wrote it. And yet without the lyrics, a country music song would merely be a country music tune. To all the writers in Nashville (and wherever else they may be): Thanks for providing us with the best stories in all of music!

A few notes to our readers:

Every effort has been made to ensure the accuracy of the song titles and the answers in this book. We have listened to hundreds of CDs and thousands of hours of radio as part of the research for this book; however, with 450 questions, it is possible that we may have erred once or twice (although we certainly hope not). Our apologies in advance for any word(s) that we may have misinterpreted or misquoted in the preparation of this trivia collection.

Although some country songs listed in this book were previously recorded by other musical artists, we usually mention the country singer who most recently released that particular song. Sometimes, but not always, we will mention that the song is a remake (otherwise known as a "cover").

The vast majority of the songs mentioned in this book charted somewhere between early 1980 and the end of 1998. Occasionally, however, an earlier classic is thrown in just to keep you on your tappin' toes!

Finally, whenever statistical information is provided (e.g., that a song was number one for four straight weeks), that information is based on *Billboard*'s country singles chart. There are other industry charts that may differ slightly from the one compiled by *Billboard*.

Special thanks

Bret Nicholaus wishes to thank:

Pastor and pedal steel guitar player Matthew Marohl, for his "classic country" contributions to this trivia project. Without Matthew's help, great names like George Jones, Charley Pride, and Patsy Cline (to name a few) may not have made their way into this book.

His wife, Christina, for her wonderful love, help, and support.

Paul Lowrie wishes to thank:

Scott Kooistra and the entire gang at KKYA/ KYNT radio in Yankton, South Dakota, for access to their invaluable CD library.

Sherry, Wade, Todd, Megan, Holly, and Jenny for being a sounding board on this project, and Melva for those great Sunday dinners.

Both authors would like to thank their agent, Joseph Durepos, as well as Cathy Repetti, Mark Rifkin, and Betsy Flagler at Ballantine Books for their help with this book.

Questions

1. In the **Collin Raye** hit "Little Rock," a man moves to Arkansas to get a new start in life. Where does he work once he gets there and what does he sell?

2. In the same **Collin Raye** hit, what is the name of the church whose preacher the man likes?

3. In one of **George Strait**'s earlier hits, "Amarillo by Morning," in what Texas city does the song's character have his saddle stolen?

4. In "Song of the South," an **Alabama** staple, the main character talks about his daddy taking a job with the TVA. After he takes this job, what two items does Daddy buy?

5. In **Garth Brooks**' "Much Too Young (To Feel This Damn Old)," his debut top-ten hit, the main character mentions that he has a worn-out tape of which male country singer?

6. In "Down at the Twist and Shout," a huge **Mary Chapin Carpenter** hit with a Cajun sound, what type of stew and what type of pie are mentioned?

7. According to the same song mentioned above, a waltz from what year will make you feel a little bit young again?

8. In **Shania Twain**'s "Love Gets Me Every Time," what was "the plan" at the start of the song?

★ ★ ★

9. The father, daughter, and son trio, **The Wilkinsons**, had an extremely popular hit with their debut single, "26 Cents." As the song's 18-year-old girl rides a bus out of her hometown of Beaumont, what two things does she watch fade behind her?

★ ★ ★

10. At the end of the **Alan Jackson** hit "Livin' on Love," what is it that the aged wife can barely do anymore?

★ ★ ★

11. The very beginning of the **Trisha Yearwood** song "Everybody Knows" mentions the number of consecutive mornings the main character has woken up without her lover beside her. How many mornings has it been?

★ ★ ★

12. In "Holdin'," a **Diamond Rio** hit, the young couple can barely afford their little white house that sits on how much land?

★ ★ ★

13. The **Bellamy Brothers** describe the perfect woman in their hit "Redneck Girl." According to the song, where does a redneck girl have her name?

14. Megastar **Shania Twain**'s breakthrough hit "Any Man of Mine" is a fun, rollicking song about women having the upper hand in relationships. According to the song, what should a man's response be when a woman burns his dinner black?

15. In the **Brooks and Dunn** song "Boot Scootin' Boogie," a hit that spent four weeks at number one, what is the dance floor hotter than?

16. In "Fancy," a popular **Reba McEntire** song, the girl's mother spends every last penny she has to buy her 18-year-old daughter something special; what is it?

17. In the same Reba McEntire song just mentioned, the teenager's mother hands her daughter a heart-shaped locket with something engraved on it; what does the engraving say?

18. In the **LeAnn Rimes** song "One Way Ticket," which direction is the train headed?

19. In the debut **Terri Clark** hit "Better Things to Do," what popular afternoon talk show is mentioned?

20. In the up-tempo **Sawyer Brown** song "Some Girls Do," what late Hollywood star does the song's main character imitate for his girlfriend?

21. In the same song mentioned above, what object—which the girl twirls—is hanging in the car the couple is in?

22. In the first stanza of the popular **Alan Jackson** song "Gone Country," we learn of a woman who wants to pack up her things in Las Vegas and give the Nashville scene a try. Admitting that she's a simple girl, where does she say she grew up?

23. In "Be My Baby Tonight," sung by **John Michael Montgomery**, the man combines a cowboy word with a word from Shakespeare to describe what he's *not* trying to be. What is the description?

24. The song "In a Week or Two," by **Diamond Rio**, is about a man who procrastinates on some important issues just a little too long. After she gives up on him, what two things does the man say he would've brought the woman in a week or two?

25. In the **Randy Travis** song "The Hole," what is the song's main character driving into the ground?

★ ★ ★

26. In **Joe Diffie**'s hit "Texas Size Heartache," how tall is the blue-eyed beauty who gives the song's main character a Texas-sized heartache?

27. In the same **Joe Diffie** song mentioned above, in what Texas city does the woman leave her man?

28. What is the title of the early **Garth Brooks** hit in which a husband second-guesses whether his wife would know how much he loved her were he to die during the night?

29. In **Alabama**'s hit "Roll On (Eighteen Wheeler)," in what state does the highway patrol find Daddy's rig jackknifed in a snowbank?

30. In the **Mary Chapin Carpenter** hit "Passionate Kisses," the song's main character asks for a lot of seemingly simple things. Specifically, what does she want with regard to pens?

31. A household country name in the late eighties was **Lee Greenwood**. In Lee's hit "Holdin' a Good Hand," a song that uses gambling as an analogy for relationships, what gambling term is used to describe something a family man might desire in life?

32. Billy Ray Cyrus' megahit "Achy Breaky Heart," a song that spent five weeks at number one, includes the names of many different family members. What is the name of the aunt that the song's main character mentions?

33. In the same song mentioned above, the main character makes it clear that he can handle anything as long as it's not a heartbreak. What does he say with regard to the dog?

34. Which late-eighties **George Strait** hit takes its title from the color of the girl's eyes in the song?

35. In **Joe Diffie**'s huge hit "Pickup Man," the song's character uses a pickup truck—instead of a pickup *line*—to attract the opposite sex. According to the song, what part of a pickup truck gives off a romantic glow?

36. In the **Trace Adkins** song "Every Light in the House Is On," what type of lights does the front walk look like?

37. **Charley Pride**'s best-known song is "Kiss an Angel Good Mornin'." In the song, we are told not only to kiss an angel good morning, but also to do what when we get back home?

38. **Collin Raye** had a big hit with his song "Little Red Rodeo." What color is the car the song's character is chasing and what state's plates are on the car?

39. In one of **Alan Jackson**'s earliest hits, what type of car (which happens to be part of the song's title) is the song's character going to buy and then cruise up and down the road?

40. In the **Pam Tillis** song "Shake the Sugar Tree," what is jealousy as bitter as?

41. In the **Mary Chapin Carpenter** hit "I Feel Lucky," how much money does the woman in the song win in the lottery?

42. In the same song mentioned above, two well-known country singers happen to be in the bar where the woman goes after she wins. Who are they?

43. What is the title of the **Clay Walker** hit whose main character figures out how he could be a millionaire in a week or two?

44. In the **Travis Tritt** song "T-R-O-U-B-L-E," the song's main character was one of how many kids that his mama did her best to raise?

45. In the song "Whose Bed Have Your Boots Been Under," an early **Shania Twain** hit, many women's names are mentioned. What is the name of the redhead down the lane?

46. In **Tim McGraw**'s debut smash, "Indian Outlaw," the song's main character has what two types of Indian blood?

47. In **Trisha Yearwood**'s hit "XXX's and OOO's" (also known by the title "An American Girl"), the girl in the song has a picture of her mama wearing what two things?

48. According to the **George Strait** song "True," what are the odds, in this modern world, of two lovers ever making it to forever?

49. In the **Doug Stone** song "Jukebox with a Country Song," a man goes to a country bar after a fight with his wife only to discover that the former one-room tavern has recently undergone a major change. What does he immediately notice about the barroom floor?

50. In "A Little Too Late," sung by **Mark Chesnutt,** a man finds that he is just a little too late to do the things that might have saved his relationship. Spending late hours away from the house didn't help any; what time does the main character say he came home last night?

★ ★ ★

51. In the upbeat, optimistic **Jo Dee Messina** song "I'm Alright," what class of income does the song's main character fall into?

52. In the same **Jo Dee Messina** hit just mentioned, what is the person wearing who comes to visit the woman?

53. In **Trisha Yearwood**'s song "Perfect Love," where do the man and woman drink their morning coffee?

54. In the beautiful duet "Just to Hear You Say That You Love Me," sung by **Faith Hill** and **Tim McGraw**, what would the character be willing to go and capture "just to hear you say that you love me"?

55. In the **Dan Seals** hit "Bop," the guy in the song tells the girl that he wants to take a ride in her car. What kind of car does she own?

★ ★ ★

56. Randy Travis had one of the biggest country hits of the eighties with "Forever and

Ever, Amen," which held the top spot for three weeks in 1987. According to the song, old men love to talk about the weather; what is it that old women love to talk about?

57. In **The Judds**' hit "Have Mercy," where was the main character standing in line at the start of the song?

58. In the **Tim McGraw** song "One of These Days," what is the name of the teenage small-town beauty that the guy walks away from after promising her the world?

59. In "All My Ex's Live in Texas," an early hit from **George Strait**, a man leaves Texas to get away from all the previous women in his life. In what state does he decide to settle?

60. Four ex's are mentioned in the song listed above, as well as the Texas city that each woman resides in. Can you name at least three of the women and the corresponding city?

61. In **Garth Brooks**' song "Two Piña Coladas," what is the name of the captain with whom the main character says that they should set sail?

62. In **John Michael Montgomery**'s "Life's a Dance," what one physical feature do we know about the girl in the main character's homeroom class?

63. In **Tim McGraw**'s song "Don't Take the Girl," the victim of a holdup starts offering personal possessions to the robber. One thing he offers him is a watch. Who does he say gave him that watch?

64. In "What the Heart Wants," by **Collin Raye**, a man and woman strike up a conversation at three o'clock in the morning. Where does this conversation—which lasts until dawn—take place?

65. A big **Alabama** hit, whose title is the song's first line, was "If You're Gonna Play in Texas (You Gotta Have a Fiddle in the Band)." The song makes it clear that a lead guitar may be hot, but *not* for a man from what state?

66. In the **Tanya Tucker** song "Ridin' Out the Heartache," what is the year and type of car that the main character is driving?

67. In the beautiful love song "In This Life," sung by **Collin Raye**, what does the man say he was once imprisoned by?

68. Brooks and Dunn had a big hit in the fall of 1998 with their remake of Roger Miller's song "Husbands and Wives." What does the main character believe is the chief cause in the decline in the number of husbands and wives?

★ ★ ★

69. In **Alan Jackson**'s song "Don't Rock the Jukebox," the main character admits that his heart isn't ready for the Rolling Stones. On the other hand, what country singer does he *want* to hear?

★ ★ ★

70. According to the same song listed above, what musical instrument is the best for drowning a memory?

★ ★ ★

71. In a hit off of **Garth Brooks**' *Sevens* album, the song's character asks a certain object to let go of his hand. What is the object and thus the song's title?

★ ★ ★

72. Australian-born country singer **Sherrie Austin** had her first big hit with "Lucky in Love." When it comes to men, the song's character is waiting to be dealt a "King of Hearts" but keeps getting what other card instead?

★ ★ ★

73. In the same hit just mentioned, the girl is taken on a date to a Dairy Queen restaurant. What does the guy from Paris, Tennessee, buy her there?

74. In **John Berry**'s first release, "Kiss Me in the Car," in what year does the main character say that he bought his '65 Mustang?

75. In **Neal McCoy**'s "The Shake," a song about being more attracted to the right moves than to the right looks, 10 different cities are rattled off in a row during the song's climax. One of the 10 locations mentioned is somewhere in Florida; what is it?

76. In the same song mentioned above, two biblical characters are mentioned. Who are they?

77. In **Sammy Kershaw**'s "Meant to Be," a man and a woman meet by chance in the Dallas/Fort Worth Airport and ultimately end up spending the rest of their lives together. What gate number do they meet at?

78. Again, call it fate, the two characters above who meet at the airport happen to be from the same city. What city are they both from?

79. In "Sittin' on Go," a **Bryan White** hit about a man who is ready to start a relationship as soon as his would-be love gives him the go-ahead, how quickly does he say he could be hers?

80. What popular **Trisha Yearwood** song served as the theme song for the movie *Con-Air*?

81. One of **Lorrie Morgan**'s songs, "Go Away (No, Wait a Minute)," is all about a woman who can't make up her mind. According to the woman in the song, how many times does she have a right to change her mind?

82. "Friends in Low Places," a song originally pitched to George Strait, became one of **Garth Brooks'** biggest hits. What are the three types of alcohol that are mentioned at one time or another during the song?

83. In the **Hank Williams, Jr.** hit "All My Rowdy Friends Are Coming Over Tonight," what does the main character warn that you had better not step on?

84. Deana Carter's debut smash hit was "Strawberry Wine," a song that catapulted her into country stardom. The woman in the song, reflecting back on her younger days, remembers thinking that what age was old?

* * *

85. According to the same **Deana Carter** song mentioned above, how old was the woman when she got her first taste of love?

* * *

86. "Strawberry Wine" deals with a woman's youthful summers spent on a farm. In her younger days, what month was the woman's biggest fear?

87. In **Roger Miller**'s big hit "King of the Road," what does two hours of pushing a broom buy?

88. What **Clint Black** song begins and ends with the sound of rain?

89. What **Clint Black** song, which sizzled at number one for three weeks, mentions the words *heat wave*, *day in the sun*, and *makin' that tan*?

90. In **Brooks and Dunn**'s hit "That Ain't No Way to Go," a woman writes a good-bye note to her boyfriend, but not with the traditional pen and paper; what two objects does she use to write her letter?

91. In the **Suzy Bogguss** song "Drive South," what does the main character tell her boyfriend that she's not going to pack for the trip?

92. In **Tanya Tucker**'s "It's a Little Too Late," the woman wants something turned up and something thrown down; what are those two things?

93. **Willie Nelson** had a hit with "City of New Orleans." According to the main character who hops on a train, how far will he have gone before the day is done?

94. A well-known song from **Shenandoah** could have been titled "24 Flowers with Thorns on Them"; however, it probably wouldn't have had the same impact. What is the real title of this song?

★ ★ ★

95. In **Deana Carter**'s "I've Loved Enough to Know," what has the woman loved enough to know?

96. In **Clint Black**'s "Wherever You Go," a song talking about the dead-end street of alcoholism, what liquor is mentioned in the opening line of the song?

97. In the **Trisha Yearwood** song "Wrong Side of Memphis," what type of car is going to get the girl to her dreams in Nashville?

98. In the same **Trisha Yearwood** hit mentioned above, what interstate is the girl in the song going to travel down to get to Nashville?

99. In **Collin Raye**'s "I Think About You," a song about a dad's love and concern for his little girl, how old is the daughter?

100. In the beginning of the same song just mentioned, what product is the woman on the billboard trying to sell?

101. In **Alabama**'s song "Dixieland Delight," where is the couple going to do a little "turtle doving"?

102. In **John Michael Montgomery**'s "Cover You in Kisses," what city is mentioned with "a foot of new snow on the ground"?

103. In **Ricky Van Shelton**'s song "Don't We All Have the Right," we all have the right to be what?

104. **Toby Keith**'s debut release, "Should've Been a Cowboy," roped the top spot and held it there for two weeks. In the hit, what two famous TV cowboys does the main character mention?

★ ★ ★

105. In "My Kind of Girl," **Collin Raye** sings of two people who apparently have a lot in common. The girl makes a big "hit" with the guy when she mentions that even through the rotten years she was a fan of what baseball team?

★ ★ ★

106. In the same song mentioned above, what two magazines does the man see the woman buying?

★ ★ ★

107. Again, in "My Kind of Girl," a famous writer, a famous political leader, and a famous movie star are all mentioned. Who are these three people?

★ ★ ★

108. In **Alabama**'s "Jukebox in My Mind," what is the sound that the listener hears at the very beginning of the song?

★ ★ ★

109. In **Patsy Cline**'s "Walking After Midnight," what type of tree does the love-struck character stop to see?

110. In the **Marie Osmond/Dan Seals** chart-topping duet "Meet Me in Montana," what does the main character say that she wants to see in her lover's eyes?

111. In **Diamond Rio**'s "Meet in the Middle," their debut song that stayed at number one for two weeks, how many fence posts was it between "your house and mine"?

112. In the same song mentioned above, under what type of tree did the couple say their wedding vows?

113. An early **Garth Brooks** hit was "Two of a Kind, Workin' on a Full House." According to the main character, what is his wife's limousine?

★ ★ ★

114. In **Brooks and Dunn**'s "Hard Workin' Man," a biblical reference is used in the song's refrain. What is it?

★ ★ ★

115. The setting for **Steve Wariner**'s mid-eighties hit "Small Town Girl," ironically, is America's largest city. Which street does the song say is covered with a foot of snow?

★ ★ ★

116. On two different occasions, **Johnny Cash**'s "Folsom Prison Blues" was released. What crime does the main character commit, where does it occur, and why does he say that he did it?

★ ★ ★

117. In **John Anderson**'s "Seminole Wind," the main character talks about standing on a cypress stump in the swamp and hearing whose ghost cry out?

★ ★ ★

118. In the **George Strait** hit "Adalida," what feat would the main character perform just to stand beside his sweet Adalida?

119. In the **Jo Dee Messina** song "You're Not in Kansas Anymore," what famous Malibu, CA, resident does the song's character inquire about?

120. Diamond Rio's "Imagine That" is a song about a couple that intends to defy the odds and make their love last forever . . . but what does the man say he *doesn't* intend to do (and couldn't do even if he tried)?

121. In the **Bryan White** song "Rebecca Lynn," where did Rebecca Lynn grow up?

122. In the same **Bryan White** song listed above, what was the big event happening on the night that the guy proposed to Rebecca Lynn?

123. In the song "The Thunder Rolls," one of **Garth Brooks**' most popular, what time is it at the very beginning of the song?

124. In "Walkaway Joe," sung by **Trisha Yearwood** with a little help from Don Henley, a teenage boy and girl run away together; but early in their escape the boy pulls into a gas station and robs it clean. In what city does this robbery take place?

★ ★ ★

125. In the **George Jones** classic "He Stopped Loving Her Today," what year are the love letters dated that the main character keeps by his bed?

★ ★ ★

126. In the **Wade Hayes** song "The Day That She Left Tulsa," the main character stands on a bridge as he watches his lover driving away; what does he see flashing in the passing lane?

127. In **Garth Brooks**' "Rodeo," a song about a man seemingly more in love with the rodeo than with his lover, what would the woman give for her man to change the way he feels?

128. In **Randy Travis**' first number-one hit, "On the Other Hand," what is it that's on the other hand?

129. In **Toby Keith**'s song "We Were in Love," what does the main character wish he could invent?

130. In "Then You Can Tell Me Goodbye," a great remake by **Neal McCoy**, what does the main character want to have sweetened with a morning kiss?

131. According to the lively **Vince Gill** hit "What the Cowgirls Do," there are cowgirls all across this country. What northeastern city is mentioned in the song?

132. In what part of what city does the main character drink her problems away in the **Emmylou Harris** song "Two More Bottles of Wine"?

133. In **Travis Tritt**'s debut hit, "Country Club," what is the name of the road that leads past the pool and the 18th green?

134. Which women's fashion magazine receives mention in **Martina McBride**'s first big hit, "My Baby Loves Me (Just the Way That I Am)"?

135. What is the title of the early **Alan Jackson** hit that mentions a certain kind of rainbow?

★ ★ ★

136. A popular remake by **Billy Dean** talks about a couple who "can't see eye to eye." They don't share the same opinion, but rather than get upset they simply accept that fact. What is the title of this song and thus the fact that they willingly accept?

137. Randy Travis had an early hit with a song entitled "Deeper Than the Holler." What two types of birds are mentioned in the song's refrain?

138. In **Mary Chapin Carpenter**'s hit "I Take My Chances," the woman in the song is listening to a TV preacher who promises to show his viewers "the way" in return for their personal checks. In defiance, the woman flips the channel back to CNN and does what else?

139. In **Lonestar**'s popular song "Everything's Changed," a small town has seen a lot of progress in recent years; in fact, everything has changed except for a man's love for an old sweetheart. What does the man tell his ex-lover that they have built on the site of the old drive-in?

***

140. In "Drink, Swear, Steal, and Lie," sung by **Michael Peterson**, what does the main character intend to steal from his sweetheart?

141. In **Mindy McCready**'s song "A Girl's Gotta Do (What a Girl's Gotta Do)," what was the very first thing the girl did when her boyfriend said good-bye?

142. In the same song mentioned above, what was the very *next* thing the girl did?

143. **Chely Wright** and **Mary Chapin Carpenter** share something in common: They both had big hits with songs that have the word *shut up* in their title. What are those two songs?

144. **John Anderson**'s hit "Somebody Slap Me" is all about a woman who is, quite simply, perfect in every way (if only in the eyes of the man in the song). Where does this woman have a diploma from?

145. In **Trisha Yearwood**'s hit "The Song Remembers When," the couple in the song was "rolling through the Rockies" when a radio station in a certain city played "that song." In what city was the station located?

146. In **Alabama**'s "Down Home," a song that held the top spot for three weeks in 1991, what are the old men in the hardware store gathered around?

147. "Live Until I Die" was a hit for **Clay Walker** early in his career. What two things did the man in the song like to skip as a child?

148. In **Steve Wariner**'s CMA award–winning song "Holes in the Floor of Heaven," the young boy's grandma dies the day before his birthday. How old is he going to be?

★ ★ ★

149. In **Tracy Byrd**'s huge hit "Watermelon Crawl," what is the name of the county in which the watermelon festival is taking place?

150. In the same **Tracy Byrd** song mentioned above, who gives the welcome speech at the start of this small-town festival?

151. Patty Loveless had an early hit with "I'm That Kind of Girl." At the start of the song, what is the man wearing who's standing outside the woman's window?

152. The **Collin Raye** song "That's My Story" is a collection of excuses that a man gives his wife for why he wasn't with her. His first excuse is that he fell asleep; *where* does he say that he fell asleep?

153. Referring to the question above, what did the wife recently do that made his story refutable?

154. In "From a Jack to a King," another **Ricky Van Shelton** hit, the main character goes "from loneliness to" what?

155. **Tim McGraw**'s "Everywhere" is a song about a lovesick man who seems to see his old sweetheart everywhere he goes. What does he think he sees her doing in Albuquerque?

156. In the same **Tim McGraw** song mentioned above, the man apparently sees his long-lost sweetheart watching a sunset where?

* * *

157. In **Wynonna**'s song "Rock Bottom," the main character takes a most optimistic outlook on being down on her luck. In her positive approach to life, how does she view a dead-end street?

* * *

158. One of **Shenandoah**'s most popular songs mentions barbecued chicken and the *TV Guide*. What is the title of this song?

159. In **Garth Brooks**' "What She's Doing Now," according to the last information that the main character had heard, where had his ex-girlfriend moved to?

160. In **Trisha Yearwood**'s "Everybody Knows," everybody seems to know what the heartbroken woman in the song should do except the woman herself. She says that she doesn't want a shrink and she doesn't want a drink, but what two things does she *want* to be given?

161. In the **Suzy Bogguss** hit "Give Me Some Wheels," while the man in the song was looking for the words to make the woman stay, what was *she* looking for?

162. Doug Stone's hit "In a Different Light" is a song about a man who falls for a woman who works in the same office as he does. How far away from him does she sit?

163. In the **Pam Tillis** song "I Said a Prayer," what type of tree is mentioned?

164. In **Diamond Rio**'s controversial hit "It's All in Your Head," what specific revelation does the boy's stepmama receive regarding the Kennedy assassination?

165. In the same song mentioned above, how does Daddy—who's a sidewalk soapbox preacher—die?

166. In the **George Strait** song "You Can't Make a Heart Love Somebody," the refrain tells us that "you can lead a heart to love but you can't" what?

167. In the song "Love Without End, Amen," a **George Strait** hit that stayed at number one for five weeks, a young boy gets sent home from school for getting into a scuffle. What physical proof is there that the boy has indeed been in a fight?

168. In **Hank Williams'** hit "Hey, Good Lookin'," the main character tells a woman that he has a Ford and what denomination of currency?

169. At the start of the song "How Can I Help You Say Goodbye," a **Patty Loveless** hit, what is the name of the little girl whose friend is moving away?

★ ★ ★

170. In one of **Patty Loveless'** earlier huge hits, "Blame It on Your Heart," the main character uses seven different adjectives to describe her not-so-wonderful lover's heart. Can you name at least six of those descriptive words?

171. What is the title of the **Restless Heart** hit that mentions the words *long stretch of blacktop, white lines*, and *city limit signs*?

172. **Suzy Bogguss**' beautiful but sad song "Letting Go" is about moving away and moving on in your life. In the first verse of the song, the girl who's leaving for college grabs the painting hanging in the hallway. At what time in her life did she paint it?

173. In **Clint Black**'s song "State of Mind," what is it that can bring back a memory and change your state of mind?

★ ★ ★

174. **Jeannie C. Riley** sang the popular late-sixties hit "Harper Valley P.T.A." This classic song is about a Harper Valley widowed wife and her teenage daughter who attends Harper Valley Junior High; what is the widow's name?

★ ★ ★

175. An early **Billy Dean** hit reminds us that when it comes to love, there's something you don't do. What is this song's title and thus the admonishment of what you don't do?

176. In **Tim McGraw**'s hit "Just to See You Smile," the main character's ex-girlfriend left Amarillo to take a new job in what state?

177. "Check Yes or No," one of **George Strait**'s all-time biggest hits, is a song about a couple's lifelong love for each other. According to this chart-topper, in what grade of school did this relationship start?

178. In the same song mentioned above, the schoolboy gets his first kiss and then is told by the young girl not to tell anyone. Where are the two kids when this kiss takes place?

179. Although **Reba McEntire** is generally known for more serious love songs, she had a

fun hit with "I'd Rather Ride Around with You."
What church is the main character's cousin
getting married in?

180. In this same **Reba** hit, where are the
bride and groom going for their honeymoon?

181. In the **Wynonna** song "Girls with Guitars," to what famous chain store does the girl's
father take her to buy her first guitar?

182. Throughout one of **Tanya Tucker**'s greatest hits, "Strong Enough to Bend," a couple's
solid love for each other is compared to what
large object?

183. In the **Tracy Lawrence** song "If the
Good Die Young," the constable clocks the
main character going how fast?

184. In the **Sawyer Brown** song "The Boys and Me," the boys are high on life and low on what?

185. "Not That Different," sung by **Collin Raye**, is a song about the many feelings that all of us share in life. Eight specifics are mentioned in the song's refrain, one of them being "I laugh." What are five of the remaining seven?

★ ★ ★

186. **Alabama**'s popular song "Cheap Seats" is a song about baseball—and the things that go with it. According to the main character, how do he and the people in his town like their beer?

★ ★ ★

187. In **The Judds**' Country Music Awards Single of the Year "Why Not Me," the main character questions a man about why he is looking everywhere for the right love when she is right there waiting for him. Apparently the man is looking a little *too* far away from home; what foreign location does the main character mention?

188. In **Pam Tillis**' "Mi Vida Loca (My Crazy Life)," using a flower as a metaphor for herself, what kind of flower does the main character say can't be tamed?

189. Which **Alabama** hit takes its title from a large river that flows in the southern part of the country?

★ ★ ★

190. In **Randy Travis**' "Out of My Bones," the man in the song does everything he can to put his ex-lover out of his mind . . . but he can't quite let go. Where does he now carry her picture?

191. A big hit from **Alan Jackson**'s first album was also the album's title: "Here in the Real World." According to this song, which contrasts life on the silver screen to what goes on in the real world, what two things *don't* happen in the movies?

192. In a huge hit from **David Lee Murphy**, "Dust on the Bottle," who makes a wine like no one else?

193. "I Swear" was a huge hit for **John Michael Montgomery**. What metaphor is used by the song's main character for what he and his lover will hang on the walls?

194. In **Reba McEntire**'s "The Fear of Being Alone," what does the man "order up" while he and the woman are sharing their respective stories?

195. In **Martina McBride**'s "Independence Day," where do the firemen send the young girl?

★ ★ ★

196. In the same **Martina McBride** song mentioned above, how old was the girl "that summer" when the tragedy occurred?

197. In **Faith Hill**'s hit "Let's Go to Vegas," what will the couple bet on?

198. The title of **Trace Adkins**' first hit single tells of something in Texas. What is there in Texas?

199. In **George Strait**'s song "You Know Me Better Than That," a hit that stayed at the top position for three weeks, what magazine does the main character catch his girlfriend paging through?

* * *

200. **Deana Carter**'s song "Did I Shave My Legs for This" tells the story of a woman who has become very frustrated with the lack of attention she receives from her husband. When she comes home, two things make it perfectly clear that she won't get so much as a kiss. What are those two things?

* * *

201. The title for one of **Rhett Akins'** hits mentions something that the main character sees at his girlfriend's house that belongs to another guy. Seeing it makes it clear to him that their relationship is over. What is the title of this song?

202. The classic **Alabama** hit "Forty Hour Week (For a Livin')" is a tribute to the hardworking men and women across the nation. In the song, three distinct areas of the country are mentioned: Detroit, Pittsburgh, and Kansas. What is the job of each person thanked in these three geographical locations?

203. One of **Mark Chesnutt**'s funniest songs is "Bubba Shot the Jukebox." With what *does* Bubba shoot the jukebox?

204. In the same song mentioned above, what was the name of the place where this incident occurred?

205. In **Pam Tillis'** "All the Good Ones Are Gone," how old will the woman turn "this weekend"?

206. An **Alan Jackson** hit early in his career was "Midnight in Montgomery." The song pays tribute to somebody else who had quite a nice, but brief, career of his own. Who is the song about?

★ ★ ★

207. "She Don't Know She's Beautiful" is a **Sammy Kershaw** hit about a girl who under-estimates her own beauty. In the song, when does the woman think she looks her worst (yet her husband can't take his eyes off of her)?

208. In **Billy Ray Cyrus'** hit "It Could've Been Me," the main character learns that an ex-girlfriend recently got married. According to the information he was told, how long was her honeymoon?

209. According to **Merle Haggard**'s anti-hippie anthem "Okie from Muskogee," what two items will never be seen in Oklahoma?

210. In **Mark Chesnutt**'s "Goin' Through the Big D" (which stands for *Divorce*), what does the main character get out of the divorce and what does his ex-wife get?

211. In the same song mentioned above, in what month was the wedding and in what month was the divorce?

212. In **Shania Twain**'s "No One Needs to Know," a woman plans her entire future without telling a soul—including the man she expects to have as her future husband! In planning her family, she says that they'll have a little girl, a little boy, and a little dog. What does she say that they'll name that dog?

★ ★ ★

213. In **Terri Clark**'s "Poor, Poor Pitiful Me," what namebrand kitchen gadget is mentioned?

214. In **Alan Jackson**'s "Dallas," a title based on the name of the woman in the song, where does he wish Dallas was?

215. In the 1980s hit by **Reba McEntire** "Whoever's in New England," in what city is the main character's husband having an affair?

216. In "Mirror Mirror," sung by **Diamond Rio**, what question does the person in front of the mirror continually ask?

217. In **Garth Brooks**' "Unanswered Prayers," where do the main character and his wife run into his old high-school flame?

218. In **Alan Jackson**'s hit "Chattahoochee," a song that spent four weeks in the top spot, the boys down by the river talk about one thing and dream about something else. What do they *talk* about and what do they *dream* about?

219. In **Clay Walker**'s hit "What's It to You," what does the main character hear singing?

220. In **Tracy Byrd**'s "Big Love," the main character says that his love is as endless as what?

221. In the duet "Heart Half Empty," sung by **Ty Herndon** and **Stephanie Bentley**, what is the couple's love compared to throughout the song?

222. In **Dwight Yoakam**'s classic hit "Guitars, Cadillacs," what is the third thing mentioned that immediately follows the words *guitars* and *Cadillacs*?

223. Lorrie Morgan's "Except for Monday" is a fun song about a woman who feels bad about a love gone wrong virtually every day of the week. What day of the week does she "feel better just for spite"?

224. "Old Enough to Know Better" was a huge single for **Wade Hayes**. In the song, what does the man have in his hand when he wakes up Monday morning?

225. What **Diamond Rio** hit takes its full title from the name of the woman in the song?

***

226. Shenandoah's first number-one hit was "The Church on Cumberland Road." In the song, a man is trying to get to the church for his wedding, but has been out partying all night. The driver of the car he is in has obviously had a little too much to drink; how fast is he going?

227. In the same song just mentioned, what does the groom-to-be say that his bride-to-be is sweeter than?

228. In the famous **Ronnie Milsap** hit "Smoky Mountain Rain," the main character thumbs his way from L.A. back to what other city?

229. What is the general setting for the **Deana Carter** hit "We Danced Anyway"?

230. "Blue" was the song that got **LeAnn Rimes** off to a golden start. What time of the morning is it when the girl says that she's sitting there so lonesome she could cry?

★ ★ ★

231. In **Mary Chapin Carpenter**'s song "Shut Up and Kiss Me," what does the woman in the song say that she didn't expect to have to rise above?

232. A huge hit off of **Doug Stone**'s first album was "I'd Be Better Off (In a Pine Box)." What state is the train carrying the pine box bound for?

233. Faith Hill's first hit, "Wild One," mentions a young girl sitting on her daddy's knee— a girl who is told by Daddy that she can be anything that she wants to be. How old is she when he tells her these prophetic words?

234. In **Trace Adkins**' "I Left Something Turned on at Home," what is it that he has left turned on at home?

* * *

235. In the classic **Randy Travis** song "Diggin' Up Bones," what does the lonely, melancholy main character say that he is "resurrecting"?

* * *

236. In "Summertime Blues," sung by **Alan Jackson**, the main character makes an appeal for help to his congressman. What does his congressman tell him?

237. What is the **Suzy Bogguss** hit whose story takes place in an airport?

238. In the **Doug Stone** hit "Why Didn't I Think of That," the main character tells about his ex's new lover who does everything right. The new lover "brings her roses" and what else?

239. In **Alabama**'s super hit "Give Me One More Shot," the main character mentions two U.S. cities; what are they?

240. In **Garth Brooks**' "Ain't Goin' Down ('Til the Sun Comes Up)," what famous country singer do the girl and guy listen to while they're dancing cheek to cheek?

241. The refrain of "How Your Love Makes Me Feel," by **Diamond Rio**, mentions something in the road that the car swerves to the left to avoid. What's in the road?

242. In **Mary Chapin Carpenter**'s hit "He Thinks He'll Keep Her," a man goes through life happy with his marriage simply because his wife lives up to his expectations for her. Then one day when she's 36, she meets him at the door and says something; what does she say?

243. In "There Goes," an **Alan Jackson** tune about a man who keeps falling helplessly for his sweetheart, the main character says that he should be out fishin'. What type of fish does he say he should be out fishin' for?

★ ★ ★

244. **Alabama**'s "I'm in a Hurry (And Don't Know Why)" reminds all of us of the importance of slowing down in our lives. In the song, the main character admits that he—and the rest of us for that matter—really only has to do two things; what are they?

245. In the same song mentioned above, how fast does the main character say that his car can go from 0 to 60?

246. According to "No Time to Kill," sung by **Clint Black**, what is the highest cost of living?

247. **Joe Diffie**'s "Third Rock from the Sun" is a song in which one crazy event leads to another. Where does the mayor say that the police chief is hiding from his wife?

248. In the beginning of **Lari White**'s hit "That's My Baby," what is the boy wearing when he's walking down the street?

249. In **Brooks and Dunn**'s "How Long Gone," what phrase does the man use to describe the amount of time it's been since he's seen his lover?

250. In the megahit duet "It's Your Love," sung by **Tim McGraw** and **Faith Hill**, what time is it when the couple is "dancing in the dark"?

251. Besides "Bubba Shot the Jukebox," **Mark Chesnutt** had another popular song whose title had the word *jukebox* in it. What was the title of that song?

252. In the classic **Charlie Daniels Band** hit "The Devil Went Down to Georgia," what is the name of the young man with whom the devil makes a bet?

253. **Chris LeDoux**'s "Cadillac Ranch" was a hit about a family that took the barn on an unproductive farm and turned it into a popular and successful bar. In the beginning, when things started to go bad on the farm, what two things went dry?

254. In the same song mentioned above, where do the patrons park their cars after the bar in the barn opens up?

255. In **Holly Dunn**'s hit "Daddy's Hands," the now-grown-up girl recalls how, no matter what, there was always love in her daddy's hands. When she'd done wrong, however, she remembers that his hands were as hard as what?

256. In the popular **Nitty Gritty Dirt Band**'s "Fishin' in the Dark," what are the two people in the song doing while they're lying on their backs?

257. In the same hit mentioned above, what does the couple see "floating on the breeze"?

258. A big hit that **George Strait** remade talks about a "little, bitty, teeny, weeny thing." What is that thing and thus the title of the song?

259. In **Tim McGraw**'s megahit "I Like It, I Love It," a song that spent more than a month at the top of the chart, how much money does the main character spend at the county fair?

260. In the same song mentioned above, the new girlfriend has such an effect on the man that he finds himself doing things he never did before. One of the things he mentions doing is holding umbrellas; what are the other three things?

★ ★ ★

261. In "Somewhere Other Than the Night," a **Garth Brooks** hit, a farmer comes in from the field to find his wife standing in the kitchen wearing only one piece of clothing; what is she wearing?

★ ★ ★

262. Lorrie Morgan's late husband, **Keith Whitley**, had a hit that dealt with a singer in a bar falling in love with a woman in the crowd. The title of the song is also the distance that the two are separated from each other during the gig. What is it?

263. In "The Big One," sung by **George Strait**, what does S.O.S. mean "in this situation"?

264. In **Faith Hill**'s "Someone Else's Dream," a young woman vows to make her life her own before her next birthday, i.e., within one year. How many candles are on the woman's birthday cake *this* year?

265. In the **Mark Wills** song "Don't Laugh at Me," a song that challenges all of us to attain a higher standard, why doesn't the little girl smile?

266. **Joe Diffie** popped onto the scene with his hit "Home." As the main character reflects back on his years growing up, what song does he say that Mom would sing as she hung out the clothes?

267. George Strait's "Carrying Your Love with Me" was a late nineties hit for the living legend. From what state to what other state does the main character travel in the song?

268. What is the title of the **Shania Twain** hit in which listeners hear the sound of a slamming door at the end of the song?

269. Gary Allan had a hit with "It Would Be You," a song in which many different things are compared to the main character's emotional state. According to the lyrics, if it were a color, what color would it be?

270. In **Brooks and Dunn**'s "Rock My World (Little Country Girl)," what type of car does the girl drive?

271. In the same **Brooks and Dunn** song just mentioned, what pop music singer does the girl act like and what country music singer does she like to listen to?

272. In **John Michael Montgomery**'s energetic chart-topper "Sold (The Grundy County Auction Incident)," a man falls in love with a woman at a county auction. What row is the blond-haired, blue-eyed lady sitting in when the man realizes he's "sold" on her?

273. In "A Good Run of Bad Luck," sung by **Clint Black**, who does the man in the song say he's going to have to pay if he's betting on a loser?

274. In "My Maria," a huge **Brooks and Dunn** chart-topper, the main character says that his lover sets his soul free like what?

★ ★ ★

275. In the **Keith Whitley** hit "I'm No Stranger to the Rain," a Country Music Awards Single of the Year winner, what does the main character say that he is a friend of?

276. In the same song mentioned above, what does the same man say that he is going to "beg, steal or borrow" a little of?

277. In the punchy **Garth Brooks** song "Callin' Baton Rouge," how often does the main character stop to make a call to his lover in Baton Rouge?

278. What is the woman's name in the song mentioned above?

279. In "Billy the Kid," a song that reflects youthful innocence, singer **Billy Dean** recalls his childhood days when he would play "cowboy." As he played around the neighborhood, what was his only fear?

280. The story within the spirited **Garth Brooks** hit "Papa Loved Mama" has a funny— but tragic—ending. In the end, where is Mama and where is Papa?

281. In the song mentioned above, Mama gets lonely and starts fooling around. According to the lyrics, "she needed more to hold than just a" what?

282. Again, in "Papa Loved Mama," how does the husband ultimately commit the horrible murder?

283. What is the **Alabama** hit whose three-word title consists of two pronouns and a conjunction?

***

284. In **Aaron Tippin**'s moral hit "You've Got to Stand for Something," the main character talks about how, as a boy, his family always had plenty just living his father's advice. That advice begins "Whatever you do today . . . "; what is the second part?

285. In **Lorrie Morgan**'s "What Part of No (Don't You Understand)," a song that stayed at number one for three weeks, a man in a bar doesn't seem to get the hint that the woman isn't interested in him. Knowing what he wants, she makes it clear to him that she's not into what?

286. In **Tracy Lawrence**'s song "Time Marches On," where, specifically, is Daddy at the end of the song?

287. In **Kathy Mattea**'s "Eighteen Wheels and a Dozen Roses," a Country Music Awards Single of the Year, how many miles are left on the truck driver's final four-day run?

★ ★ ★

288. In the same hit just mentioned, what is the retired couple going to buy before they "set out to find America"?

289. In **Ricochet**'s big hit "Daddy's Money," where is the main character sitting when he realizes that the girl is looking at him?

290. In **Pam Tillis**' "Cleopatra, Queen of Denial," the main character sees her boyfriend out dancing with a girl who's wearing something not considered to be country attire. What is the dancing girl wearing?

291. In **Lonestar**'s hit "No News," the main character gives a list of reasons that might explain why he hasn't heard from his exgirlfriend; what does he say that she might have accidentally locked herself in?

292. In a popular **Little Texas** hit, the main character in the song has apparently been sent to "spread the message." What is the message and thus the title of this song?

293. In **Joe Diffie**'s "Prop Me Up Beside the Jukebox," the main character asks to be propped up beside the jukebox when he dies. Furthermore, he asks to be set up with a mannequin, but reminds his friends of a physical feature he'd like the mannequin to have; what is it?

294. In the song mentioned above, the main character makes an unusual request that he'd like fulfilled upon his death: He wants his boots filled up with sand . . . and what does he want placed in his hands?

295. **Mark Chesnutt**'s first big hit was "Too Cold at Home." While it may be cold at home, he makes it clear that it's too *hot* to do what two activities?

296. In **Aaron Tippin**'s "There Ain't Nothin' Wrong with the Radio," how many speakers does the main character have across the back dash?

297. What **Confederate Railroad** song's title mentions two people who will always love you, no matter what?

298. In **Toby Keith**'s "Big Ol' Truck," what is written on the side of the woman's truck?

299. What is the name of the plain-looking girl in **John Berry**'s song "She's Taken a Shine"?

300. In **Sammy Kershaw**'s "Cadillac Style," what two famous actors does the main character say that he ain't?

301. In "John Deere Green," a huge hit for **Joe Diffie**, on what object does the main character write his love message?

302. In the same hit just mentioned, what is the message that the young man writes?

303. Dolly Parton had an early-eighties hit with her single and movie theme song "9 to 5." In the beginning of the song, the main character tumbles out of bed and stumbles to the kitchen; once there, what does she pour herself a cup of?

304. In **Alan Jackson**'s "Who's Cheatin' Who," a fun song about not being able to trust anyone, what question does the main character ask regarding a car?

305. Patty Loveless had an early hit with "Chains," a song that tells of a woman's inability to pull herself away from her husband. Where does the woman buy a ticket to, only to find that ultimately she can't get on the plane?

306. In **Brooks and Dunn**'s "Neon Moon," where is the run-down bar located?

307. In **Vince Gill**'s humorous song "One More Last Chance," a wife takes away her husband's car keys in hopes of keeping him at home and away from his good-timing buddies. With the car keys gone, what does the husband use instead to get away from the house?

308. In the **Pam Tillis** song "Maybe It Was Memphis," what famous American novelist is mentioned?

309. What is the title of the **Reba McEntire/ Vince Gill** duet that uses the words *alibi* and *foolish disguise*?

310. In **Alan Jackson**'s hit "I'd Love You All Over Again," what "just keep adding up"?

311. **Tracy Lawrence** had a hit whose title, if it were a reality, would probably require the purchase of more than 5 billion rocking chairs. What is the title of this hit?

312. In **Wynonna**'s hit "I Saw the Light," the main character spots her man with another woman and her eyes are opened to the truth. Later in the song, she tells the man to take his cheating hands off the dress she's wearing. What color is that dress?

313. In **Sawyer Brown**'s remake of "Six Days on the Road," what city does the trucker pull out of at the start of the song?

★ ★ ★

314. In the song just mentioned, what two trucks does the main character say that he just passed?

315. In **Tracy Byrd**'s "Lifestyles of the Not So Rich and Famous," who is featured on the family's TV tray?

316. In the same song mentioned above, what takes the place of champagne and caviar for this family?

317. In **Neal McCoy**'s "You Gotta Love That," the girl rolls into town in a car of what color and make?

318. "The Shoes You're Wearing" was a big hit for **Clint Black**. According to the message the song wishes to impart, "The shoes you're wearing don't" what?

319. According to the title of a well-known song from **Ricochet**, what is love stronger than?

320. In **David Kersh**'s "Goodnight Sweetheart," a man's thoughts turn to his wife as he travels on an airplane. How high above the ground is the plane flying?

321. **Waylon Jennings** had a hit television theme song about a couple of good ol' boys, a song that he both wrote and sang. What is the name of the TV show on which this song was heard weekly?

322. In **Tracy Lawrence**'s hit "Is That a Tear," what piece of electronic equipment plays a prominent part in the story?

323. In "What Mattered Most," an early hit for **Ty Herndon**, in what year and in what city was the main character's ex-lover born?

324. In what **Lee Roy Parnell** hit is the main character's lover giving him "cardiac arrest"?

325. In **Patty Loveless'** "You Can Feel Bad (If It Makes You Feel Better)," what does the woman tell her ex that he should picture her reading if he wants to feel bad?

326. In the **Kathy Mattea** hit "She Came from Fort Worth," what were the girl's dreams bigger than?

327. "Something That We Do," a song **Clint Black** wrote in honor of his wife, talks about a picture that Clint can see clearly in his head. What is the picture in his mind's eye?

* * *

328. In **Joe Dee Messina**'s hit "Bye Bye," what highway number does the woman speed down as she leaves her boyfriend behind?

329. In **Alabama**'s classic "Mountain Music," the main character says that they'll float on down the river in order to get to what?

330. In one of **George Strait**'s classics, "Baby's Gotten Good at Goodbye," a woman leaves a man just as she's done countless times before. This time, however, she doesn't do something that she always did in the past whenever she would leave; this leads the man to believe that she's gone for good this time. What doesn't she do?

331. In the **Shania Twain** hit "You Win My Love," the main character mentions a bunch of different vehicles that she considers to be sexy; of course, she would hope that any guy she goes out with would have one of these. What special feature does she want the cool Cadillac to have?

* * *

332. In **Mark Chesnutt**'s classic "All My Old Flames Have New Names," the man in the song mentions a lot of former girlfriends who are now married. According to the man, "the wildest lover of my life" is now the wife of what?

333. In **Tim McGraw**'s "Can't Be Really Gone," a man walks into his sweetheart's bedroom and tries to use the clues in the room to convince himself that his lover hasn't walked out. He discovers a book she was reading and finds that she is currently in the midst of what chapter?

334. In the same song mentioned above, the woman has marked the spot in her book with a playing card; what number and suit is the card?

335. In **The Statler Brothers**' classic "Flowers on the Wall," what TV show is being watched by the cigarette-smokin', heartbroken man?

336. In **Alan Jackson**'s song "Wanted," whom does the main character call with the hope that she can help him?

337. In "Love's Got a Hold on You," an **Alan Jackson** hit, who does the main character call for some help?

338. In **Mark Chesnutt**'s "Blame It on Texas," the main character finds a way to blame his problems on, well, Texas! In hearing the song, where do we learn that the man lived as a boy?

339. In the **Marty Robbins** classic "El Paso," what is the name of the place where nighttime finds the love-struck main character?

340. Johnny Paycheck's classic "Take This Job and Shove It" is about a disgruntled worker who has finally had enough and leaves his job at the factory. How many years had this man worked at the factory?

341. In **Lee Greenwood**'s famous and patriotic "God Bless the USA," what is the northernmost state mentioned in the song?

342. In the **Sawyer Brown** song "Thank God for You," the main character runs down a list of people—and institutions—that he'd like to thank for getting him to where he is. One person he thanks is his mama, for the cookin'; immediately after that, what does he thank Daddy for?

343. In **Lee Ann Womack**'s melodious tune "A Little Past Little Rock," what city does the woman leave in the beginning of the song in order to get away from the memories of her now-ex-lover?

★ ★ ★

344. In **Lorrie Morgan**'s hit "Half Enough," the main character says that she wishes that there were a big room somewhere; what does she want kept in that big room?

345. In **Martina McBride**'s title song from her third album, "Wild Angels," what does the woman in the song swear she hears?

346. In **Tracy Byrd**'s debut hit "Holdin' Heaven," the main character has been waiting all night to do something with the girl in the song; what has he been waiting for?

347. What is the title of the **Tim McGraw** hit that Ralph Kramden (of *The Honeymooners*) would have really appreciated? (Hint: Think of one of Ralph's famous lines.)

348. In **Brooks and Dunn**'s big hit "Brand New Man," the main character says that he's been baptized by two things, neither of which is water. What are those two things?

★ ★ ★

349. In "Is There Life Out There," **Reba McEntire** sings about a girl who married a man and "thought she was ready" when she was how old?

350. A big hit off of **Shenandoah**'s debut album was "Sunday in the South." In the song, the preacher at the church is shaking hands with the parishioners while he grips the Bible in the other hand. The word *Bible*, however, is not used; what metaphor is used in its place?

351. **Marty Stuart** had a huge hit with "Hillbilly Rock." Referring to this kind of music, the song states that some say that it came from Memphis, down in Tennessee; but others say that it drifted in from Georgia—in what year?

352. In **John Michael Montgomery**'s song "Cowboy Love," the main character tries to make a country convert out of a truly upscale type of girl. What type of car does this girl drive?

353. In **Dwight Yoakam**'s "A Thousand Miles from Nowhere," what does the main character say that he's got in his pocket?

354. Someone in the **Collin Raye** hit "One Boy, One Girl" says the word "congratulations" to a man and woman. Who says that word and why does he say it?

355. In **Toby Keith**'s "A Little Less Talk and a Lot More Action," a man gets himself to a bar to try to find a bit of the wild side. When he arrives there, he spots a good-looking woman sitting at a corner table; what mundane activity is she engaged in when he first spots her?

★ ★ ★

356. "I Wanna Go Too Far," sung by **Trisha Yearwood**, is a song about a conservative woman who's tired of playing it safe in life. According to the song, why does she want somebody to draw the line?

★ ★ ★

357. According to a popular mid-eighties hit from **Steve Wariner**, what do lonely women make? (Hint: Guess the title of this song and you've got the answer.)

358. In **Aaron Tippin**'s "That's As Close As I'll Get to Loving You," what's the closest (in terms of physical contact) that the main character ever gets to the woman who works with him?

359. In the **Lorrie Morgan** song "Five Minutes," she tells her significant other that something is on its way; what is it that's about to arrive?

360. One of **Reba McEntire**'s earlier hits was "Little Rock." In this particular instance, what is the title actually referring to?

361. In **Dan Seals**' "Everything That Glitters (Is Not Gold)," the main character spots his ex's picture on a rodeo poster in a café. In what city is this café located?

362. In "Heads Carolina, Tails California," sung by **Jo Dee Messina**, which coin is flipped to decide where the song's duo will travel?

363. "If You've Got Love" was an early hit for **John Michael Montgomery**. According to the song, if you've got love in your heart, what can you turn an ordinary picture into?

364. In **John Anderson**'s "Straight Tequila Night," what is the letter/number combination of the woman's favorite jukebox song?

365. Two big hits by **Clint Black** have some real "sole" to them. Which two of his songs have the word *shoes* in the title?

★ ★ ★

366. In **Tanya Tucker**'s beautiful song "Two Sparrows in a Hurricane," the story is told of a couple who stay together their entire lifetime— even though the odds are against them. At the beginning and end of the song, when he is very young and very old, what is the man barely doing?

367. In **Clint Black**'s fun, up-tempo hit "Nothin' But the Taillights," what two-word phrase does the main character use to describe where he was sitting in the car before his gal dropped him off on the side of the road and let the gravel fly?

368. In **Vince Gill**'s super hit "Don't Let Our Love Start Slippin' Away," the main character tells his sweetheart that "a wounded love walks a real thin line." He then adds that there's something that will kill that love every time; what is it?

★ ★ ★

369. In **Brooks and Dunn**'s rockin' song "Little Miss Honky Tonk," the main character says that he wouldn't give up his sweetheart for a thousand of something; what wouldn't he give her up for?

370. In the **Tracy Lawrence** song "Texas Tornado," the main character says that his lover is playing him like a certain instrument; what instrument is it?

371. The Kentucky Headhunters had a fun hit with their song "Dumas Walker." Once the group gets down to Dumas Walker's, what three things are they going to order?

372. According to a huge **Alabama** hit, what is burning in the woman's eyes that "tears can't drown and makeup can't disguise"? (The answer is the title of the song.)

★ ★ ★

373. **David Kersh** had a big hit with "If I Never Stop Lovin' You," a song about a man so much in love that he fumbles his words in front of his girlfriend. He admits to her that he did something in front of the mirror earlier in the day. What did he do?

374. In **Garth Brooks**' "That Summer," a song about a heated summer affair between a young man and a much-older woman, how far "from nowhere" are the man and woman?

375. In **Alabama**'s "Born Country," how many years of "down home" does the main character say is running through his blood?

376. In the same **Alabama** hit mentioned above, the main character recalls a food in his mamma's kitchen; what is it?

377. **Tim McGraw** stayed at number one for four weeks with his smash hit "Where the

Green Grass Grows." While expressing his disdain for urban living, what does the main character say is growing in the city park?

378. A well-known **Rick Trevino** song takes its title from the name of the girl the song's character sat behind in high school. What is the girl's, and thus the song's, name?

379. In **Collin Raye**'s "That Was a River," the main character's feelings for an old love are compared to a river; what are the feelings for his new love compared to?

380. "Small Town Saturday Night," sung by **Hal Ketchum**, deals with weekend life for teenagers in a small town. Everybody in the song is broke except for Bobby. How much money does he have and what does he do with the money?

★ ★ ★

381. In the playful song "Before You Kill Us All," sung by **Randy Travis**, exactly where are the goldfish?

382. In **Pam Tillis'** beautiful song "Let That Pony Run," a woman named Mary moves to West Virginia to start her life over. Once she's there, she gets a divorce . . . as well as a horse. What is the color of that horse?

383. "I Want to Be Loved Like That" was a big hit for the group **Shenandoah**. In the song, what two deceased silver-screen stars are mentioned?

384. The **George Strait** hit "Blue Clear Sky" talks about falling in love before you know what hit you. According to the main character, one day you're giving up a dream, and what are you doing the next day?

385. In **Faith Hill**'s "This Kiss," what two fairy-tale characters are mentioned?

386. A fun **Garth Brooks** song mentions an organization you should join if "your conversation calls for something more than a coffeepot"; what is the full name of this organization and thus the title of this hit?

387. In **Ty Herndon**'s heartfelt song "Living in a Moment You Would Die For," what does the main character say that the inscription on his stone should say when he dies?

388. In a popular song by **Alan Jackson**, the following 14 things are all preceded by the same adjectives: house, yard, dog, car, baby, gown, town, books, look, check, world, plan, dream, and scheme. What are the two small words used to describe all of the above and is also the title of the song?

★ ★ ★

389. Joe Diffie had a humorous hit with "If the Devil Danced in Empty Pockets." In the song, the gullible main character goes to an advertised car sale only to find that all the cars in the lot are gone. The salesman, however, tells the man that for a little cash he's got something for him out behind the barn. What does he have for him behind the barn?

390. In the early **John Anderson** hit "Swingin'," what is the name of the girl who's swingin' on the front porch with the main character?

391. The Kentucky Headhunters had an unusual hit with "Trashy Women." In the song, the main character shows by his actions that he likes his women a bit on the unsophisticated side. When he introduces his parents to his prom date, they are quick to point out that she is actually a cocktail waitress; what type of wig is she wearing?

392. In **Tracy Lawrence**'s hit "That's How a Cowgirl Says Goodbye," what well-known gas-station chain receives mention?

393. **Willie Nelson** and **Waylon Jennings** had a huge hit with their duet "Mammas Don't Let Your Babies Grow Up to Be Cowboys." After warning mothers not to let their babies become cowboys, what professions do they encourage mammas to let their babies pursue?

394. **Kenny Chesney**'s "She's Got It All" was a hit that talks about a man who believes he has found the perfect woman. In the beginning of the song, the man says that his sweetheart has "every quality from (what?) all the way to (what?)"?

395. **Barbara Mandrell** had a super hit with "I Was Country When Country Wasn't Cool." Can you fill in the blanks? "They called us (what?) for stickin' to our roots."

* * *

396. In "Tall, Tall Trees," sung by **Alan Jackson** (and written by George Jones and Roger Miller), a man tries to say all the right things to impress a woman. In talking to the woman, what does the man say that he'll give his utmost attention?

397. The **Dixie Chicks** had an early mega-hit, "Wide Open Spaces," that spent four weeks at the top of the charts. In the song, a young woman seeks independence and the chance to make her own life away from her parents. But worried dads will be worried dads; when the girl's parents visit her for the first time, what does her dad yell from the car as he and Mom are about to drive away?

398. An early **George Strait** hit was "Ocean Front Property." According to the main character, if you believe that he's got ocean-front property in Arizona, what will he throw in for free?

399. **Kenny Rogers**' huge hit "The Gambler" uses poker as a metaphor for life. In this song, two men talk as they ride a train; where is the train bound for?

400. In **Alan Jackson**'s fun, up-tempo hit "I Don't Even Know Your Name," what is the good-looking waitress doing the first time the main character spots her?

401. In the same song mentioned above, the man gets wasted in the restaurant and ends up accidentally asking the wrong waitress to marry him. What type of drink does he order that precipitates this big mishap?

***

402. **Tammy Wynette** often claimed that the 1968 hit "D-I-V-O-R-C-E" was her personal favorite of her many chart-toppers. In this song, a couple on the verge of divorce spells out words to keep the pain from their four-year-old son. What is their son's name, which is also spelled out in the song?

403. In a big hit from **Ty Herndon**, "I Want My Goodbye Back," the main character wishes, in hindsight, that he hadn't ended the relationship with his sweetheart. His doctor asks him for his ex's phone number; what does the man give the doctor instead?

404. In "It Sure Is Monday," a **Mark Chesnutt** hit, the main character takes a nap in what, for most people, would be a rather unusual location; where does he take this nap?

405. In **Collin Raye**'s multiweek chart-topper "Love, Me"—a song about not giving up on the one that you love, in life or death—a principal character in the story dies. From the young boy's point of view, who is that person?

406. In a popular **Trisha Yearwood** hit, a woman calls up her love in the middle of the night to tell him something very simple. What is the title of the song and thus the words she speaks on the phone?

407. In **Tennessee Ernie Ford**'s hit "Sixteen Tons," what does the main character say that you get when you load sixteen tons?

408. In **Diamond Rio**'s hit "Walkin' Away," what still fits even after all this time?

409. In **Vince Gill**'s "Whenever You Come Around," what does the main character in the song say that he is "standing here holding"?

410. In **The Judds**' hit "Grandpa (Tell Me 'Bout the Good Old Days)," we are reminded of something that families used to do; what is it?

411. In "High Cotton," a song that went high on the charts for **Alabama,** what does the main character admit was the hardest thing he ever faced?

412. "Carried Away," sung by **George Strait**, is a song about a man who's flying high since he met the love of his life. He compares the way he feels about her to something flying in the sky on a windy day; what is it?

413. In **Neal McCoy**'s "No Doubt About It," the main character talks about many classic combinations to describe to his lover how perfectly matched the two of them are. He says that the two of them are meant to be together—like coffee and a cup, a hammer and a nail, socks and shoes. What perfectly matched musical combination does he mention?

414. According to the title of one of **Ricky Skaggs**' eleven number-one hits (a hit from 1983, to be exact), what type of blues has the main character got?

415. In the **Trisha Yearwood** debut hit "She's in Love with the Boy," what are the names of both the girl and the boy in the song's story?

416. In the same **Trisha Yearwood** song just mentioned, the boy can't afford to buy a wedding band yet; what does he give the girl in its place?

417. In the **Patty Loveless** hit "I Try to Think About Elvis," what type of bar does the main character try to think about?

418. In the **Tim McGraw** hit "Down on the Farm," what is it, on Friday nights, that leads to a field filled with pickup trucks?

419. In a huge hit from **John Berry**, what is the main character standing on the edge of? Hint: Guess the title and you'll get the answer.

* * *

420. One of **Kenny Rogers**' all-time greatest hits, "Coward of the County," offers words of wisdom from a father to his son. What is the son's, and thus the coward of the county's, name?

421. In the famous **George Jones** song "White Lightning," the boy asks his pappy why he doesn't use the more popular word for bootlegged alcohol; what is that term?

422. **Mark Chesnutt**'s hit "Thank God for Believers" is about an alcoholic's wife who stands by him through it all. According to her husband, what is she stronger than?

423. In **Reba McEntire**'s number-one hit "The Heart Is a Lonely Hunter," a man in the bar says, "Hey, can I buy you a drink?" As soon as he says this, the woman sees something; what is it?

424. In "Why Haven't I Heard from You," **Reba McEntire** mentions the name of a famous inventor; who is it?

425. In the **Patty Loveless** song "She Drew a Broken Heart," the woman draws a broken heart on the man's satin sheets using a tube of lipstick. What was the brand and the color of the lipstick used?

426. Mel McDaniel's first top-ten hit was "Louisiana Saturday Night." What is unusual about the dog in this song?

427. David Ball is probably best known for the song "Thinkin' Problem." The first three words of the song, which are repeated again later in the same fashion, are sung without any instrumental accompaniment and are immediately followed by a distinct drumroll. What are these three words?

* * *

428. Very early in the nineties, the **Oak Ridge Boys** had a big hit with "No Matter How High." What number does the main character say that he's willing to settle for?

429. **Hal Ketchum**'s song "Mama Knows the Highway" is about a woman trucker who knows the road like the back of her hand. According to the song, how can Mama tell that she's in Wyoming?

430. In the rockin' **George Strait** hit "Heartland," you know you're listening to the sound of the American heart when you hear what three instruments?

431. A huge early-nineties hit from **Randy Travis** was "Look Heart, No Hands." With his tennis shoes up on the handlebars, the main character used to ride his bike down a hill. What was the name of the hill?

432. In **Joe Diffie**'s "Honky Tonk Attitude," what does the waitress never leave you with?

433. Same title, different message. Both **Reba McEntire** and **Collin Raye** had huge hits with a song that has the same title, but that is where the similarity ends; the lyrics are *completely* different. What is the song title that earned both stars hit records?

434. In **The Judds'** song "Give a Little Love," the woman makes it clear that love is more important to her than how her man looks or where he's from. In fact, as far as she's concerned, he could wear a pointed hat and be from what country?

435. **Billy Dean**'s breakout hit was entitled "Only Here for a Little While." According to the main character in the song, what particular event did he attend earlier in the day?

436. In **Suzy Bogguss'** "Hey Cinderella," what is the color and type of car in which the newlyweds drive away?

437. The **Pam Tillis** song "Spilled Perfume" is about a woman who thought she had found a man whose love would last forever; instead, it lasted only one passionate night. After the fact, she has an indisputable look on her face that her friend easily recognizes. What does the friend call that look on her face?

438. The **Vince Gill** hit "When I Call Your Name," a Country Music Awards winner, is about a man whose wife walks out on him without any warning at all. The note that the man's wife left on the table said that she had grown weary of something; specifically, what was it?

439. In **Clint Black**'s "When My Ship Comes In," a song that sailed to the top of the charts and anchored there for two weeks, where is the main character going to sail out of?

440. In the highly energized **Shania Twain** hit "Honey, I'm Home," a woman comes home from work and demands many of the same things that some men traditionally expect of their wives: get off the phone, pour me a cold one, get me something to eat, etc. What does the woman tell the man to do with regard to the dog?

441. In **John Michael Montgomery**'s "I Love the Way You Love Me," a hit that spent three weeks at number one, the main character makes it clear that he likes even the most simple things about his sweetheart . . . including how she enjoys her long baths. How long are the baths that she takes?

442. Early in **Garth Brooks**' song "You Move Me," a comparison is made between life and therapy. According to this hit, in what two ways are life and therapy alike?

443. **Ty Herndon**'s fast-moving hit "It Must Be Love" is about a man who is beginning to think that his relationship with his gal might be approaching a new level—love! In the beginning of the song, the main character admits that he should be flying (high on love) but instead he's sitting somewhere, pondering this new feeling. Where is he sitting?

★ ★ ★

444. **Shelly West** and **David Frizzell** received the 1981 Country Music Award for Vocal Duo of the Year, thanks to a huge chart-topper that was featured in the film *Any Which Way You Can*, starring Clint Eastwood. What was the title of that song?

445. **Faith Hill**'s hit "Let Me Let Go" is about a woman who, try as she might, just can't get an old love out of her mind. Two different times, in the song's chorus, the woman mentions how many miles she's been down a dead-end road. How many is it?

446. In "Someone You Used to Know," the beautiful but sad song from **Collin Raye**, the man mentions something that he and his ex-lover used to argue about . . . then follows it up by saying, "Well, I guess I won that one" (referring to the argument). What exactly did the couple used to argue about?

★ ★ ★

447. In **Clay Walker**'s catchy song "You're Beginning to Get to Me," the main character doesn't want to admit that he's in love . . . yet he shows all the signs that he is. Where does he have his girlfriend's picture displayed?

448. In **Shania Twain**'s hit "That Don't Impress Me Much," what is the name of the popular movie actor who is mentioned midway through the song?

449. **Tim McGraw** ended a phenomenal hit-after-hit year in 1998 with the fast-paced song "For a Little While." In the song, the man recalls how he and an old flame used to engage in a certain activity while parked on Airport Road. What was the activity?

450. In **Terri Clark**'s hit "You're Easy on the Eyes," the final number-one country song of 1998, the good-looking ex-boyfriend in the song comes knocking on the woman's door "at half past [what?], at quarter to [what?]"?

Answers

Answer to question in Introduction: Emmylou Harris

1. He works at a Wal-Mart selling VCRs

2. Church of Christ

3. Houston

4. A washing machine and a Chevrolet

5. Chris LeDoux

6. Alligator stew and crawfish pie

7. 1910

8. Staying single

9. Her high school and the house with the white picket fence

10. Sweep the floor

11. 32

12. A quarter acre

13. On the back of her belt

14. I like it like that!

15. The Fourth of July

16. A dancing dress

17. "To thine own self be true"

18. Westbound

19. *Donahue*

20. James Dean

21. Pink fur dice

22. Long Island

23. A Rhinestone Romeo

24. Diamonds and a long, long string of pearls

25. His future

26. 5'3"

27. Amarillo

28. "If Tomorrow Never Comes"

29. Illinois

30. Pens that won't run out of ink

31. A full house

32. Aunt Louise

33. "You can tell the dog to bite my leg"

34. "Baby Blue"

35. The cargo light

36. Runway lights

37. Love her like the devil

38. Candy Apple Red is the color; Texas is the state

39. A Mercury; the title of the song is "Mercury Blues"

40. A green spring berry

41. $11 million

42. Dwight Yoakam and Lyle Lovett

43. "If I Could Make a Living (Out of Loving You)"

44. Nine

45. Rita

46. Cherokee and Choctaw

47. Heels and pearls

48. Two in a million hearts

49. The sawdust is gone

50. A quarter to three

51. Middle ("I'm above the below but below the upper")

52. A three-piece suit

53. By the flower bed

54. The moon

55. A '55 T-bird

56. Old men

57. The city bus stop

58. Patty Sue

59. Tennessee

60. Rosanna in Texarcana, Ilene in Abilene, Allison in Galveston, and Dimples in Temple

61. Captain Morgan

62. She had blue eyes

63. His grandpa

64. A Laundromat

65. Louisiana

66. A '66 Chevrolet

67. The power of gold

68. Pride

69. George Jones

70. A steel guitar

71. "Longneck Bottle"

72. The Joker

73. French fries

74. '74

75. Tampa Bay

76. Adam and Eve

77. #29

78. Atlanta

79. In a second or so

80. "How Do I Live"

81. At least a couple hundred times

82. Champagne, whiskey, and beer

83. His cowboy boots

84. 30

85. 17

86. September

87. An 8-by-12 4-bit room

88. "Like the Rain"

89. "Summer's Comin'"

90. Lipstick and the mirror

91. Her nylons

92. She wants the jukebox turned up and saw-dust thrown down

93. 500 miles

94. "Two Dozen Roses"

95. A heartache when she sees one coming

96. Scotch whiskey

97. A '69 Tempest

98. 40

99. Eight years old

100. Beer

101. On the Mason-Dixon Line

102. Denver

103. Wrong now and then

104. Gene (Autry) and Roy (Rogers)

105. The Atlanta Braves

106. *Cosmo* and a hot-rod magazine

107. William Faulkner, Martin Luther King, and James Dean

108. A coin dropping into a jukebox

109. A weeping willow

110. The mountains

111. 700

112. A pine tree

113. A pickup truck

114. The Promised Land

115. Fifth Avenue

116. He shot a man in Reno "just to watch him die"

117. Osceola's ghost

118. He'd swim the Pontchartrain

119. Johnny Carson

120. Change the world

121. Carolina

122. The high-school prom

123. 3:30 in the morning

124. Abilene

125. 1962

126. The caution lights

127. Half the state of Texas

128. A golden (wedding) band

129. A time machine

130. His coffee

131. Bangor, Maine

132. West L.A.

133. Clubhouse Drive

134. *Vogue*

135. "Chasin' That Neon Rainbow"

136. "We Just Disagree"

137. The robin and the whippoorwill

138. She lights another cigarette

139. A new Wal-Mart

140. All her kisses

141. She sat herself down and had a real good cry

142. Put a red dress on and went dancing downtown until the break of dawn

143. "Shut Up and Drive" and "Shut Up and Kiss Me"

144. Beauty school

145. Jackson

146. A checkerboard

147. Rocks and rope

148. Eight years old

149. Rind County

150. The mayor

151. A Stetson hat

152. In the hammock in the yard

153. Last week she threw the hammock in the attic

154. A wedding ring

155. Waiting out a blizzard

156. In Monterey

157. It's just a place to turn around

158. "Next to You, Next to Me"

159. Boulder

160. Chocolate and a magazine

161. Her keys

162. Three desks down

163. A maple

164. That there were two shooters on the grassy knoll

165. He's bitten by a snake that the Spirit moved him to pick up

166. Make it fall

167. There's a "shiner" on his eye

168. A two-dollar bill

169. Jamie

170. Lyin', cheatin', cold-dead beatin', two-timin', double-dealin', mean-mistreatin', and lovin'

171. "Wheels"

172. When she was in junior high

173. A melody

174. Mrs. Johnson

175. "You Don't Count the Cost"

176. Tennessee

177. Third grade

178. On the school bus

179. The Methodist church

180. Hawaii

181. Sears Roebuck

182. A tree in the backyard

183. A hundred and four

184. Gas

185. I love, I hope, I try, I hurt, I need, I fear, and I cry

186. Flat as can be

187. Singapore

188. A wild rose

189. "Tennessee River"

190. In his shoe

191. Cowboys don't cry and heroes don't die

192. Creole Williams

193. Memories

194. One more bottle of wine

195. To the County Home

196. Eight years old

197. Love

198. "There's a Girl in Texas"

199. *Brides* magazine

200. The TV and beer

201. "That Ain't My Truck"

202. Detroit autoworker, Pittsburgh steelmill worker, and Kansas wheatfield farmer

203. A Colt .45

204. Margie's Bar

205. 34

206. Hank Williams, Sr.

207. In the morning, with her hair all a mess

208. A month long

209. Beads and Roman sandals

210. He gets the Jeep and she gets the palace

211. The wedding was in August, the divorce was the following June

212. Leroy

213. A Waring blender

214. In Tennessee

215. Boston

216. "Who is the loneliest fool of all?"

217. At a hometown football game

218. They talk about cars and dream about women

219. Angels

220. The stars above

221. A glass of wine

222. Hillbilly music

223. Wednesday

224. A hammer

225. "Norma Jean Riley"

226. 95 mph

227. The dew on a honeysuckle vine

228. Knoxville

229. A happy little foreign town

230. 3:00 in the morning

231. Her reputation for cynicism

232. Georgia

233. Three years old

234. His lover

235. Memories of a love that's dead and gone

236. "I'd like to help you, son, but you're too young to vote"

237. "Outbound Plane"

238. Lines he composes

239. New York and L.A.

240. George Strait

241. A cow

242. "I'm sorry; I don't love you anymore"

243. Blue marlin

244. Live and die

245. In 5.2 (seconds)

246. Dying

247. At Smokey's Bar

248. Snakeskin boots and a baseball cap

249. A month of Sundays

250. The middle of the night

251. "Brother Jukebox"

252. Johnny

253. The well and the cow

254. In the old feed patch

255. Steel

256. Counting the stars

257. Lightning bugs

258. (The) "Love Bug"

259. $48

260. Opening up doors, taking out the trash, and sweeping the floor

261. An apron

262. "Ten Feet Away"

263. She's Outta Sight!

264. 27

265. Because she has braces on her teeth

266. "Amazing Grace"

267. West Virginia down to Tennessee

268. "(If You're Not in It for Love) I'm Outta Here"

269. A deep, deep blue

270. A T-top Camaro

271. "She acts like Madonna but she listens to Merle (Haggard)"

272. The second row

273. A devil

274. A ship sailing on the sea

275. Thunder

276. Sunshine

277. Every hundred miles

278. Samantha

279. Being late for supper

280. Mama's in the graveyard and Papa's in the pen

281. Telephone

282. He drives his rig through the wall of the motel room in which his wife and her lover are located

283. "She and I"

284. "... you'll have to sleep with tonight"

285. One-night stands

286. In the ground beneath the maple tree

287. 10

288. A Winnebago

289. In church (the girl is up in the choir loft)

290. Leopardskin pants

291. A bathroom stall

292. "God Blessed Texas"

293. Blond hair

294. A stiff drink

295. Fish and golf

296. 16

297. "Jesus and Mama"

298. "In your wildest dreams"

299. Rosie

300. Burt Reynolds and Tom Selleck

301. The town's water tower

302. "Billy Bob loves Charlene"

303. Ambition

304. "Whose car is parked next door?"

305. Seattle

306. Across the railroad tracks

307. His old John Deere

308. William Faulkner

309. "The Heart Won't Lie"

310. The memories

311. "If the World Had a Front Porch"

312. Red

313. Pittsburgh

314. A Jimmy and a White

315. Elvis

316. RC Cola and a Moon Pie

317. A blue Pontiac

318. "Make the man"

319. "Love Is Stronger Than Pride"

320. 30,000 feet

321. *The Dukes of Hazzard*

322. An answering machine

323. In '64 she was born in Baton Rouge

324. "Heart's Desire"

325. The love letters he sent her

326. The Texas sky

327. Their wedding day

328. Highway 4

329. A Cajun hideaway

330. She doesn't cry

331. A Jacuzzi in the back

332. A federal judge

333. Chapter 21

334. The two of hearts

335. *Captain Kangaroo*

336. The woman who sells the classified ads at the newspaper

337. The doctor

338. In Beaumont

339. Rose's Cantina

340. 15

341. Minnesota

342. The whoopin'

343. Dallas

344. "All the time that got away somehow"

345. Beating wings

346. The chance to have one dance with her

347. "One of These Days"

348. He's been baptized "by the fire in her touch and the flame in her eyes"

349. 20

350. The Gospel gun

351. 1953

352. A baby blue Beamer

353. Heartaches

354. The doctor, because the woman gave birth to twins

355. She's peeling the label off a long-neck bottle

356. So she can blow right past

357. "Lonely Women Make Good Lovers"

358. Casually touching her hand

359. A taxi—to get her away from him

360. The diamond ring the woman is wearing

361. Phoenix

362. A quarter

363. A priceless work of art

364. K-13

365. "Put Yourself in My Shoes" and "The Shoes You're Wearing"

366. He's barely driving a car

367. "Ridin' shotgun"

368. No communication

369. A thousand buckle bunnies

370. A piano

371. A slawburger, fries, and a bottle of Ski

372. An "Old Flame"

373. He rehearsed what he would say to his girlfriend

374. A thousand miles from nowhere

375. A hundred

376. Corn bread

377. Concrete

378. "Bobbie Ann Mason"

379. An ocean

380. A buck, which he uses to put "a dollar's worth of gas in his pickup truck"

381. Floating at the top of the bowl

382. Chestnut

383. Natalie Wood and James Dean

384. Picking out a ring

385. Cinderella and Snow White

386. "American Honky-Tonk Bar Association"

387. "Once lived a man who got all he ever wanted"

388. "Little Bitty"

389. A two-tone Nash

390. Charlotte Johnson

391. A Dolly Parton wig

392. Texaco

393. Doctors and lawyers and such

394. A to Z

395. Country bumpkins

396. A great big mansion

397. "Check the oil"

398. The Golden Gate (Bridge)

399. Nowhere

400. Wiping ketchup off a table

401. Straight tequila

402. J-O-E

403. A black eye

404. In the bed of his truck

405. His grandma

406. I've been "Thinkin' About You"

407. You get another day older and deeper in debt

408. The slipper

409. The biggest heartache in town

410. "Bow their heads to pray"

411. Leaving home

412. A feather

413. Rhythm and blues

414. (The) "Highway 40 Blues"

415. Katy and Tommy

416. His high-school ring

417. Sushi bars

418. A steady cloud of dust

419. "Standing on the Edge of Goodbye"

420. Tommy

421. Mountain dew

422. The 90-proof

423. The pale white circle where he normally wears his ring

424. (Alexander Graham) Bell

425. Revlon Rose

426. It's a one-eyed dog

427. "Yes, I admit"

428. Number two

429. By the wind

430. Twin fiddles and a steel guitar

431. Two-mile hill

432. A half-empty glass

433. "Little Rock"; Reba climbed the charts with this title in 1986, and Collin did it in 1994

434. Old Siam

435. The funeral of a good friend

436. A white Mustang

437. An "I can't believe I did that" look

438. She'd grown weary of "living a lie"

439. Colorado

440. Give the dog a bone

441. Two hours

442. Real expensive and no guarantees

443. At a green light

444. "You're the Reason God Made Oklahoma"

445. Two thousand

446. About who loved who the most

447. On the dash of his new truck

448. Brad Pitt

449. They'd put the seats back and watch the planes leave town

450. At half past a heartache, at quarter to four

☆ ☆ ☆

Index

(Alphabetical listing by artists' first names; numbers refer to the question numbers, not the page numbers)

ALSO BY
BRET NICHOLAUS AND PAUL LOWRIE

Open up these books
and open up a new world
of fun and conversation

THE CONVERSATION PIECE

THE MOM & DAD
CONVERSATION PIECE

THE CHRISTMAS
CONVERSATION PIECE

THINK TWICE!

Everybody's using these books to spark
good talk

Office friends   Schools   Church groups   Families

Published by Ballantine Books.
Available in bookstores everywhere.

Read on . . .
More Country from Ballantine!

KEEPIN' IT COUNTRY
The George Strait Story

by

Jo Sgammato

Keepin' It Country explores what America loves so much about George Strait: the tremendous talent he generously shares while keeping his own life private, his authentic country life and spirit, and his renown as a true gentleman whose career is the bridge between the past and the future of country music.

FOREVER YOURS, FAITHFULLY
by Lorrie Morgan

*Lorrie Morgan was born to be
a country-western music star.*

In FOREVER YOURS, FAITHFULLY, Lorrie Morgan tells her tempestuous story of sweet triumph and bitter tragedy. From her childhood as a Nashville blueblood, performing at the Grand Ole Opry at the tender age of eleven, to her turbulent, star-crossed love affair with Keith Whitley, a bluegrass legend she loved passionately but could not save from his personal demons, to her rise to superstardom, she lays bare all the secrets and great passions of a life lived to the fullest.

And her story would not be complete without the music that has been her lifeline.

Published by Ballantine Books.
Available wherever books are sold.

*The Dazzling Rise of
a Young Country Star*

**DREAM
COME
TRUE**

THE LeANN RIMES STORY
by
Jo Sgammato

Who is this singer with the incredible voice, the
youngest artist ever nominated for a Country Music
Association Award, and winner of a Grammy Award
for Best New Artist? Find out all this and more in
this heartwarming story, complete with four pages of
color photos!

Published by Ballantine Books.
Available at your local bookstore.